Stop Talking
to Your Plants
and Listen

Stop Talking to Your Plants and Listen

By Elvin McDonald

Illustrations by Lauren Jarrett

FUNK & WAGNALLS

NEW YORK

For Mark, Steven, and Jeannene,
who have helped me learn that
parenting requires listening
perhaps more than talking

Parts of the Introduction appeared originally in the August 1975 issue of *House Beautiful* magazine. Used by permission. Copyright © 1975 by The Hearst Corporation.

Copyright © 1977 by Elvin McDonald

Designed by C. Linda Dingler

Manufactured in the United States of America

Library of Congress Cataloging in Publication Data

McDonald, Elvin.
  Stop talking to your plants and listen.

  Bibliography: p.
  Includes index.
  1. House plants—Diseases and pests.   I.   Jarrett,
Lauren.   II.   Title.
SB608.H84M3 1977   635.9′65   77-9024
ISBN 0-308-10288-6
ISBN 0-308-10333-5 pbk.

Contents

Introduction
Requiem for a Dead Palm

A long time ago, while I was in school, a friend of mine had a big palm tree that just up and died, or so he said. Two evenings later I found myself at a wake for the deceased, which had been laid out, as it were, for us to pay our last respects. Being the only person there who was of horticultural persuasion, I was asked to read from Gray's *Manual of Botany*. About halfway through the technical description of the palm's most private parts, the departed (or so we thought) rustled a frond or two, gave a slight sway away from me, then came crashing to the floor around my feet.

What I've decided since then is that my friend talked to the palm when he should have been listening. Probably the first thing the palm said after it came to live in the apartment near Columbia University in New York City was, "I've got a bad case of jet lag." In plant sign language, the palm made this perfectly clear by turning its oldest leaves from green to yellow to dead. Had my friend done his homework before adopting the palm, it might have adapted to the new environment and lived happily ever after.

Unfortunately, yellowing, dying leaves send inexperienced—and some not so inexperienced—gardeners into panic. The tendency is to overwater or underwater—or both—and the truly hyper people pour on the fertilizer, figuring if a little is good, a lot is better. If all of this fails, which it likely will if done in extremes, the plant will go on talking by turning more and more leaves yellow.

Some plants literally lose grip and shower dead leaves all over the floor.

At this point most people lose grip also. Moving the plant to more or less light seems the right thing to do—and it might be, but not before considering the plant's needs and how close the present situation comes to meeting them. In short, plants, like all other living things, suffer shock when moved from one environment to another. Even if you can duplicate exactly the original environment in your home, there is still the unknown of what may have happened to the plant in transit.

The way I cope with a new plant is to look up its needs—light, temperature, soil moisture, and humidity—in a good reference book. I do my best to keep the soil nicely moist—never bone-dry and never soggy-wet—and I withhold fertilizer until new growth is apparent. Just remember, some leaf loss is natural when you move a plant, sometimes even within the confines of a single room.

Although my experience with the dead palm left a lasting impression, this book is actually an outgrowth of much more recent experiences. About three years ago I was sent on a national media tour to promote a new book. In a period of eighteen days I visited twenty-two cities, from New York to San Francisco, and from Minneapolis to Tampa/St. Petersburg. Early on I came to the terrible realization that every interviewer was going to ask me if I talked to my plants. The only clever response I could think of that would lead to sensible conversation was to say, "No, but my plants say a lot of things to me."

"What," my host or hostess would respond, "are some of the things your plants say to you?" Well, with a question like that, I was home free, not that anthropomorphism is my thing. Plants are plants and people are people. However, communications is my business and if ascribing human traits to a plant makes its behavior more easily comprehensible, then I am satisfied to set aside such considerations.

After those hectic weeks on the road, I returned home exhausted and eagerly anticipating spending some quiet time with my plants. I found them literally crying for attention and I really couldn't blame my sitters; how could they be expected to master the needs of three hundred different plants in three weeks' time? After I had watered those that were really dry, I began a methodical examination of each plant to see what else was needed.

As I groomed each one, I consciously asked myself, what would it say to me if it could talk? Some of the gardenia leaves showed yellow between the dark green veins, a sure sign that the acid-alkaline balance of the soil was out of whack. "I'm turning yellow because I have acid indigestion," I jotted down in my notebook.

Then I found a semperflorens begonia standing with the base of the pot in a pool of foul-smelling water trapped in the bottom of a ceramic bowl with no provision for drainage. If this plant could talk, I decided it would say, "Help! I can't swim. I'm drowning!"

By the time I finished examining and grooming every plant in my apartment, I had practically filled the notebook with my interpretations of what their varied appearances and conditions had said to me. Not one complained about not having me around to talk to it or play its favorite music, but all had something important to say about the essentials for healthy growth, such as water, light, humidity, and protection from insects. Even the African violets, most of which greeted me with nosegays of bloom, had dead leaves and flowers that needed to be picked off. "A facelift would make us beautiful," I could hear them saying.

With all of this in mind, I proposed to my editor-in-chief at *House Beautiful,* Wallace Guenther, that we do an article entitled, "Stop Talking to Your Plants—and Listen!" Both Wally and Ruth Weil, the Editorial Director, responded enthusiastically and, a few months later, it became a reality in the August 1975 issue. By the time the story was in proofs, I knew that people in general would probably respond favorably, simply because of the way everyone exposed to it at *HB* reacted. But as the day of publication drew near, I felt apprehensive. What would my colleagues in the Garden Writers Association of America say? Would my more scholarly friends strike me off as unprofessional and cute? Worse, was I running the risk of offending the countless people who enjoy talking to their plants or, conversely, scoff at the very idea that communication can exist between plants and humans?

Well, I needn't have worried. The response was all favorable. One trade journal even went so far as to say that I had made a breakthrough in the communications gap between plants and people. Readers wrote that for the first time they recognized and understood the sign language of their own plants. And in time the article prompted two telephone calls of considerable importance to me. Benson Srere, vice president and general manager of King Features Syndicate, stressed how he liked the commonsense approach to growing house plants and invited me to write a syndicated column along similar lines. Now I'm in more than a hundred newspapers worldwide.

The second call came from Paul Fargis, editor-in-chief of Funk & Wagnalls. It had been almost a year since I had finished the Revised Edition of *The World Book of House Plants* for him. We had been looking for an idea for a new book about which both of us would feel enthusiastic; if I agreed, Paul said that this could be it.

My response to Paul's call is obvious, for it has become the book you hold in your hands, but it could never have become a reality without his patience and understanding in allowing me the time necessary to determine the answers to some difficult plant problems. I am also grateful to Lauren Jarrett, the artist, gardener, and friend who interpreted the appearance of complaining house plants in forty-nine sketches and then created a final fiftieth of a group expressing total content.

Although introductions to books always appear among the first pages, they are usually written last, and this one is no exception. Early on I had planned to include here a discussion about the basic needs of house plants. However, as I have neared completion of the manuscript, it has become apparent to me that all the basics and more have already been included.

In the end, *Stop Talking to Your Plants and Listen* is really a plea for common sense in dealing with members of the plant kingdom. However mysterious some of their ways may seem, all plants, but especially those we grow indoors, have very few and very simple basic needs. In most cases, these needs consist of bright light or direct sun, the temperature range of an average office or dwelling, soil that is kept between moist and nearly dry, with no long periods of extreme wetness or dryness, and thorough showering with tepid water once a month to refresh the leaves and discourage insects.

When something goes wrong with a plant, usually one or more of these basic needs is not being provided. It's that simple but, as I explain in the pages that follow, the domino principle applies: each basic need interacts with all the others. Red spider mites, for example, are not likely to make a serious invasion unless average temperatures are too high, the relative humidity is too low, and there is a lack of fresh air circulation. And, while we may blame a terminal case of root rot on overwatering, it almost invariably relates also to the amount of light, average temperature, and the general health of the plant at the time.

Once you start listening to your plants, you will discover a world of useful communication. While they might well say, "If you don't shape up, I'm going to ship out," they can also say quite affirmatively, "I like you; I just might stick around."

ELVIN McDONALD

New York City
May 1977

Fifty Talking Plants, Their Complaints, and How to Respond

In the wilds of East Africa, where the Saintpaulia was discovered almost a hundred years ago, no one could care less that the plants we know as African violets are totally unkempt: that old dead leaves and flowers are littered among the new; that hot sun following daytime rains has burned ugly spots in the leaves; or that long, reptilelike stems trail along the ground.

The domesticated African violet is quite another creature. The truth is, most of us feel better when we are well-groomed and, by the same token, we react negatively to cultivated plants that have a neglected appearance. African violets require constant grooming for the simple reason that they grow almost nonstop.

Routine grooming of an African violet consists of removing individual flowers as they begin to wither, entire stems when the last flower is gone, and mature leaves when they begin to discolor. Although young violets appear to spring directly from the soil's surface, growth actually originates from a central stem that eventually becomes exposed as more and more of the mature leaves are shed. At this stage, a violet is said to have "turkey neck."

If your violet needs a neck job, here's the procedure: Remove from pot; crumble away most of the old soil, preserving as much of the root system as possible; repot in fresh, sterilized African violet potting soil, positioning the roots deep enough so that the crown of leaves will emerge from the surface. Or, cut off the old root system, leaving about two inches of bare stem; then plant in a pot of moist vermiculite. Enclose in a plastic bag and keep out of direct sun until leaves become firm, an indication that roots have formed. Then remove the plastic and a few days later transplant to a pot of African violet soil.

All flowering potted plants, but geraniums in particular, need fertilizer with nitrogen, phosphorus, and potash in the proper balance to promote blooming. Most fertilizers for house plants are labeled as being for foliage (sometimes indicated as all-purpose) or flowering. On the container itself you will find a series of three numbers, such as 5-10-5, which always appear in the same sequence and indicate the percentages of nitrogen, phosphorus, and potash, often abbreviated NPK.

Nitrogen promotes leaf growth, while phosphorus and potash contribute to flowering, stem strength, and the nurturing of a strong root system. All things being equal, a perfectly balanced fertilizer such as 20-20-20 will give excellent results for all plants for both foliage and flowering. Geraniums simply have a greedy streak in them where nitrogen is concerned and for this reason, most successful growers recommend for them a fertilizer in a 1-2-1 NPK ratio, 15-30-15 for example, or in a ratio of 1-2-2 NPK, 5-10-10 for example.

When a flowering plant receives too much nitrogen in relation to the amount of phosphorus and potash, the common symptom is to have all leaves and no flowers. Besides the use of a fertilizer with a 1-2-1 or 1-2-2 NPK ratio, the secret to geraniums that always look like a bouquet is to give them full sun and plenty of fresh air circulation. Pot them in a mixture of three parts all-purpose potting soil to one each of sphagnum peat moss and sand; to a bushel of this mixture, add one four-inch pot of bone meal or superphosphate (or a teaspoon of either to a five-inch pot of soil). Water geraniums thoroughly, then not again until a pinch of the surface soil feels almost dry to your fingers. Soggy-wet soil leads to root rot; bone-dry soil causes old leaves and flowerbuds to die.

The fact that gardening is an inexact science is no more apparent than in matters of proper soil pH, which has to do with acidity and alkalinity. The soil pH scale runs from 1 to 14, 7.0 being neutral, figures below 7.0 being acid, those above being alkaline. Most house plants thrive in a slightly acid range of 6.0 to 6.5, and tolerate slight variances.

However, certain plants, notably citrus (including orange, lemon, lime, tangerine, grapefruit, and kumquat), azalea, gardenia, ixora, camellia, and Chinese hibiscus, have a decided preference for acidity. Without the proper amount, the leaves become chlorotic, which is to say they turn yellow.

Correcting this problem is fairly simple: make applications of micronized iron which is available in packets from nurseries, plant shops, and garden centers. Follow label instructions for rate and frequency of application. Some books recommend the use of aluminum sulfate or finely powdered sulfur, but give instructions only for the amount to apply over a hundred square feet of soil outdoors—which is not very helpful when your dwarf orange in an eight-inch pot turns yellow.

An old-fashioned home remedy for keeping acid-loving house plants healthy is to give them a cup of tea once a month. Ignore, however, the advice of anyone who tells you that a little white wine will accomplish the same thing.

It is important to use a growing medium for any of the plants mentioned above that is rich in humus, such as well-rotted oak leafmold or sphagnum peat moss. Here is an excellent recipe: three parts sphagnum peat moss to one each of all-purpose packaged potting soil and clean, sharp sand.

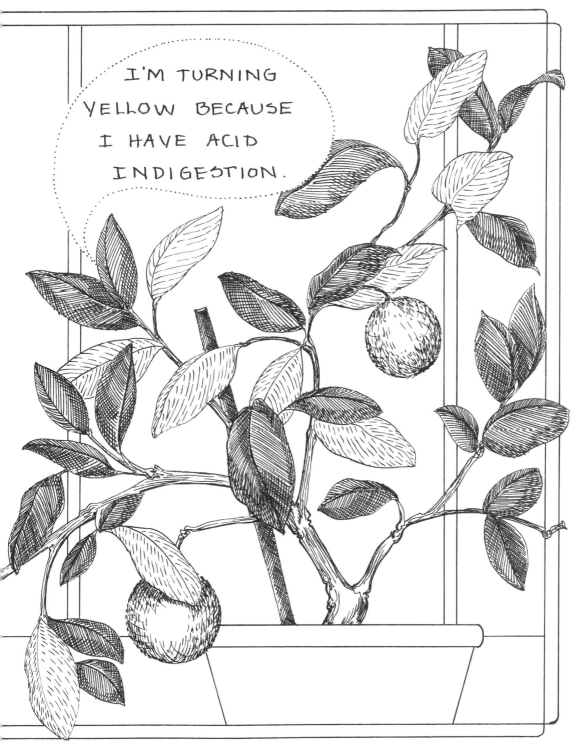

Contrary to what you may have read or been told, more plants are damaged or killed by lack of water in sufficient quantity at the right time than from overwatering. The confusion lies in the fact that visible evidence of dehydration—partially or entirely dead leaves, stems, and flowerbuds—is often not apparent for several days, weeks, or even months.

What happens is that when the soil in a pot dries out too much, parts of the root system are destroyed, thus making it impossible for the plant to assimilate water naturally. In extreme cases, the victim of underwatering is discovered dying or dead in a pot of soggy-wet soil. This often leads to the mistaken conclusion that overwatering is solely at fault.

If you've had trouble with over- or underwatering coleus, the plant illustrated here, is an excellent subject with which to experiment. It grows quickly from seeds or cuttings and wilts in an obvious manner when in need of water. Coleus also has the ability to recover quickly, usually returning to an erect, healthy appearance within an hour or two after being given a good drink of water. The only likely consequence of letting it dry to the point of severe wilting is loss of the older leaves.

If you discover a coleus or other plant suffering from bone-dry soil, immediately plunge the pot, soil and all, in a pail or basin of water and leave it to soak for a half hour or so. Meanwhile, hose down or mist the foliage. If, despite your best watering efforts, the soil dries out again and again, transplanting to a larger pot is probably in order. Herbaceous plants like coleus, Swedish-ivy, and semperflorens begonia are much more tolerant of occasional drying out than woody things such as gardenia, azalea, camellia, and English ivy.

15

When plants are moved from one environment to another, they go through a period of adjustment the same as people do. In either case, some adapt more readily than others. The weeping fig or *Ficus benjamina* shown here is typical of the plants that react noticeably and quickly when moved to a new location. In this case, the rapid loss of leaves is most likely caused by a drastic reduction in the amount of light to which the plant has been accustomed, but either bone-dry or soggy, poorly drained soil can cause the same problem, as can too much fertilizer.

What is most important about this situation is that you know your source. Experienced and caring retailers wait to sell plants trucked in from greenhouses and tropical growing areas until the shock of moving has been overcome. At Plant Specialists, Inc., in New York City, for example, ficus are conditioned to lower light levels and reduced humidity in a warehouse-turned-greenhouse by the use of row upon row of eight-foot fluorescents hung from the ceiling. Although many leaves drop in the beginning, after a few weeks the trees adapt and begin new growth, at which time they are ready to be sold.

However, no amount of conditioning can absolutely guarantee that a ficus or other plant brought into your home won't go through a further period of adjustment. In the case of a ficus, it is unrealistic to expect it to adapt to less light than that received about five feet back from a bright, sunny window.

When an established ficus begins to shed leaves for no apparent reason, check for signs of brown scale or red spider mites; be sure the soil is moist, not wet or dry. If all seems to be in order, the loss is probably natural and nothing to worry about.

The impatiens plant illustrated here is suffering from red spider mites, probably the worst insect pest presently known to attack house plants. Besides impatiens, red spider mites also show a decided preference for palm, schefflera, dizygotheca, English ivy, miniature roses and, according to underground sources, sequestered stands of marijuana.

The individual mites are hardly big enough to be seen by the naked eye, but the damage they cause en masse is readily apparent: leaves turn yellowish or gray, reddish or brown and finally the color of death, which varies from plant to plant. Individual leaves cup under and tiny webs become visible between the leaves and stems. In the case of flowering plants such as impatiens and gloxinia, the buds fall off before opening. If you suspect red spider mites, shake a branch of the plant over a piece of white paper; if mites are present, you will see dark specks moving across the surface.

Getting rid of red spider mites is no simple matter of spraying with an all-purpose houseplant insecticide. In the first place, most such products on the market are based on pyrethrin, a relatively mild poison that will kill some insect pests, but not red spider mites, which require the use of a miticide such as Kelthane or Dimite. The thing to do is *read the label*; and apply only if the product is recommended for mites.

Besides miticide sprays, there are also systemics, available in the form of granules to be applied to the soil and watered in, but neither of these can guarantee total cure unless the plant's environment is improved at the same time: Increase the amount of fresh, moist air circulation; wash the leaves and stems in tepid water at least once a week; don't let the soil dry out.

When white flies attack,
there is no mistaking their
identity. They are in fact winged,
white insects, about a sixteenth of an inch
long, that congregate, for purposes of dining,
on the undersides of leaves, especially those of
fuchsia, as illustrated here, but also clerodendrum or
bleeding-heart vine, abutilon or flowering maple, tomato,
and basil, to name a few favorites. Unless you disturb the
plant in the course of grooming, admiring, and watering it, the
presence of white flies may not be detected until sudden loss of
leaves and flowerbuds indicates that something is wrong.

Most commercially prepared all-purpose sprays for house plants
will eradicate white flies, but the best cure is to spray with syn-
thetic pyrethrum (Resmethrin). Unfortunately, the main problem is
not in finding an insecticide that will kill white flies, but rather getting them to stand still long enough to be sprayed. One effective
way to fight them is to very quietly enclose the entire plant in a
large plastic bag, leaving only enough of an opening for you to
spray through, then tie and leave overnight. Repeat at five-to ten-
day intervals as necessary.

Another way I have been successful in treating house plants infested with white flies is to gently enclose all of the plants in a large
plastic bag along with a Shell No-Pest Strip. I do this in an area
where hot sun will not shine directly on the bag and leave it sealed
for about forty-eight hours; a week later, if I can detect any live
flies, I repeat the treatment.

If white flies are present on only a few house plants, taking
them outdoors and spraying thoroughly with water from the hose
can be surprisingly effective; repeat at weekly intervals as
necessary.

Scale insects that attack house plants may be light brown or white in color, oval-shaped and about an eighth of an inch long at maturity. They are usually, but not necessarily, found on the stems and undersides of leaves. Bird's-nest fern, illustrated here, is a favorite host, but scale can be troublesome on other ferns, angel-wing begonia, palm, schefflera, dizygotheca, English ivy, gardenia, citrus, ixora, basil, and many other plants, especially kinds with glossy, waxy, or shiny leaves.

The most direct way to deal with scale is to take a soft-bristled toothbrush and some warm water with a little mild soap added and scrub away every trace of the infestation, then rinse the plant in tepid water. Work in good light and check on your thoroughness by using a magnifying glass. Repeat the treatment at weekly intervals until there is no trace of scale.

Sprays of malathion are also effective in killing scale, but not on ferns or begonias, both of which tend to be allergic to this chemical. Since hand removal of a bad attack of scale is next to impossible on ferns with leaves more delicate in texture than those of the bird's-nest, Boston for example, a third method must be used. I have been successful in using a Shell No-Pest Strip, following this procedure: I enclose the plant and the Strip in a large plastic bag, seal, and place where no sun will shine directly on it; after four or five days I remove the fern and shower the leaves in tepid water to remove as many of the dead scales as possible.

The spore cases or fruiting dots which appear on the undersides of fern fronds at certain seasons can be mistaken for brown scale, at least in some varieties. However, spore cases are uniformly distributed; scales are not and they also leave a sticky residue.

For reasons of aesthetics, most of us like to display favorite plants in cachepots, jardinieres, or other decorative containers that have no drainage holes in the bottom. There are two ways to accomplish this, one being to plant directly in the drainless container, the other, which is preferable, being to grow the plant in an ordinary clay or plastic pot of just the right size to fit inside the decorative one. In either case, the only tricky thing culturally is not to leave the plant standing for more than an hour or two in a pool of water; otherwise, the roots may suffocate.

To grow a plant directly in a container that has no drainage hole, follow this procedure: Place a layer of pebbles or gravel in the bottom, equal to about one-fourth the height of the container, then cover with a single layer of horticultural charcoal chips; proceed to add the plant and its growing medium. Add water only when the surface soil feels almost dry to your fingers and then sparingly so as not to leave the roots standing in what may become, despite the gravel and charcoal, a stagnating pool of water.

It is obviously easier to grow the plant in its own well-drained clay or plastic pot which can be placed inside the decorative container. The important rule of green thumb here is to pour off any excess moisture that collects in the bottom within an hour or two after applying water to the surface.

Whether you use the first or second method I have described, keep in mind that the roots of most house plants need air, which is why most of us place a layer of drainage material in the bottom of all containers, even when there is provision for excess water to escape. In very large pots and tubs, plastic foam pellets may be used instead of gravel to reduce the weight.

One of the most frequently asked questions about house plants is, "Why don't the new leaves of my split-leaf philodendron split the way they are supposed to?" There is no simple answer except to say that the problem is caused by several interrelated environmental factors.

First, plants of this type, most of which are not actually philodendrons but rather the related *Monstera deliciosa,* grow wild in tropical rain forests where it is their habit to creep along the ground until a rough-barked tree trunk on which to climb can be found. The air roots of the monstera firmly attach themselves to the trunk and inch upward until finally the plant grows through the top of the tree where the uppermost leaves bask in brilliant sunlight. Needless to say, the atmosphere of a tropical rain forest is usually warm and very humid.

The answer to the question, then, is to duplicate these conditions as nearly as possible if you want your so-called split-leaf philodendron to grow new leaves that are cut in the same way as those it grew before you were its keeper. Presumably your plant came not from the wilds of the tropics, but from a greenhouse where high humidity and warmth were the rule, in combination with a great deal more bright, reflected light, if not direct sun, than is present in most home and office situations where this plant is expected to grow.

Although it helps if climbing philodendrons, including the monstera, have a rough, moist surface on which to climb by means of the aerial roots, splitting is equally if not more dependent on a warm, moist atmosphere and bright light all day, preferably with a few hours of direct sun, especially in the fall and winter. It will also help to mist the leaves daily, to keep the soil moist, and to repot in fresh soil annually.

Of all the insects that strike fear in the heart of an indoor gardener, it is hard to say whether mealybugs or red spider mites are the more loathsome. If one could be more desirable than the other, I would choose mealybugs, simply because they are more readily detected before there is a serious infestation. Unfortunately, they multiply prodigiously if not checked, soon clustering on leaf undersides and along the stems, the actual mealybugs themselves swathed in cottonlike residue, as illustrated here on a gardenia.

The first thing to remember about mealybugs is that, while they favor certain plants, notably African violet, gardenia, coleus, cacti and other succulents, stephanotis, hoya, and dipladenia, hardly any plant is immune. There are even stories of neglected infestations extending beyond plants, with clusters of mealybugs, their cottony residue, and their eggs being found on draperies and in carpeting.

The second fact to bear in mind about mealybugs is that they are almost impossible to avoid entirely. Even in commercial greenhouses where pest control is a matter of routine, outbreaks of mealybugs occur. And, regardless of the treatment, followup is vital lest one egg remain viable and start the cycle all over.

The most direct means of controlling mealybugs is first to wash as many of them off the plant as possible using a brisk spray of tepid water. Allow the plant to dry, then go over it painstakingly, using a cotton swab dipped in denatured alcohol to rub off any remaining signs of the bugs; repeat this treatment every five to seven days as necessary. Sprays of malathion are also effective, but don't use this chemical in an oil base on leafy succulents such as jade plant, on begonias, or on ferns. Orthene spray will also eradicate mealybugs and some indoor gardeners have been successful in using Shell No-Pest Strips (see page 20).

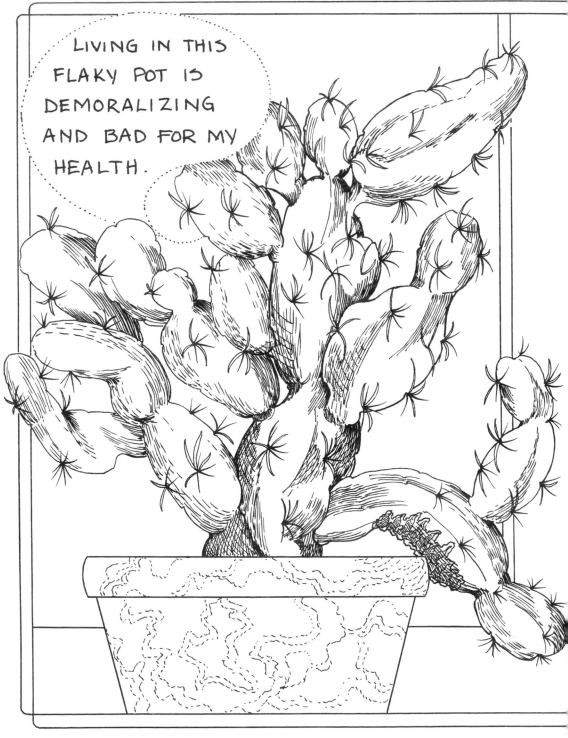

The complaint of the cactus illustrated here refers to a chalky buildup of mineral salts from water and chemical fertilizers that appears on the exterior walls as well as the rim of most pots after they have been used for a few months. The problem is most apparent on ordinary unglazed clay, but in time the buildup also becomes visible around the rims and bases of glazed pottery as well as plastic pots.

Although pots in this condition are no visual treat, the salty encrustation around the rim actually poses a serious threat to the health of any plant part that comes in direct contact with it, as illustrated by the cactus branch that has begun to die. African violet leaf stems, which are called petioles, are particularly sensitive; for this reason, some growers fold a band of aluminum foil over every pot rim, or dip the pot rims in melted paraffin at repotting time, in order to prevent petiole rot.

The solution to this problem is a simple matter of applied elbow grease with warm, sudsy water and a soap pad or stiff toothbrush. For really stubborn encrustations, it will help to use a wire brush and sometimes it may be necessary to use the tip of a knife. Obviously, it is easier to clean pots when they are empty, but you don't have to wait until repotting time. In fact, it's a lot easier to clean the pots every few months than to wait until the mineral salts have accumulated over a long period of time.

After you have scrubbed away every sign of mineral-salt encrustation from a pot, rinse in clean water. After unglazed clay dries for a few minutes, you may discover that some spots need a little more brushing. Also, if you are planning to clean empty pots, first soak them in a tub of hot water.

Housebound cats and dogs, bored by being left alone for long periods of time, can wreck a prized plant in no time. Obviously, what your pet chooses to nibble or play with is a matter of personal taste, but members of the agave and lily families are usually favored. The ones in the agave family include, besides agave, beaucarnea or ponytail, cordyline or Hawaiian ti, dracaena, sansevieria, and yucca. In the lily family, the choicest tidbits seem to be aloe and chlorophytum or spider plant, but also asparagus fern, aspidistra and haworthia. My two cats, Holly and Ivy, have also chewed on the young growth of pandanus or screw-pine and paphiopedilum or lady-slipper orchid.

One solution to the problem is to place the biggest temptations out of paw reach. Otherwise, you may unwittingly tempt your pet to nibble on something poisonous such as aglaonema or Chinese evergreen, philodendron, dieffenbachia or dumbcane, and caladium, all members of the aroid family. Another solution is to walk the dog regularly and frequently and to keep the cat's litter box clean.

I have also read advice to spray house plants with a hot pepper and water solution in order to discourage pets from nibbling. Personally, I'd rather have some chewed spider plant leaves, as shown in the illustration, than inflict discomfort on Holly and Ivy or Mitzi Beagle. At times in the past when they seemed to be eating a lot of leaves, I have relieved the problem by planting a pot of bird seed. However, now that I have more than three hundred plants in my apartment, they and the animals seem to have reached a peaceful understanding.

When a healthy plant like the gloxinia illustrated here suddenly goes limp, even though the surface soil feels moist, root rot is probably the cause. This problem is most likely to occur as a result of leaving the pot standing in a saucer of water for more than a few hours or subjecting the plant to a sudden chill while the roots are saturated with moisture. African violets, gloxinias, begonias, caladiums, and fuchsias sometimes develop root or crown rot during a period of very hot, humid weather when the soil is wet and there is little or no fresh air circulation.

If you experience sudden wilting of a plant for no apparent cause, follow this procedure: Remove the pot and crumble away the soil with your fingers, finally washing the roots clean in tepid water so that you can determine exactly the extent of damage. If, as in the case of a gloxinia, the plant grows from a bulb or tuber, check to see if it is firm or soggy and discolored. Use a sharp knife to trim off every sign of rotted or diseased tissue—leaf, stem, bulb or tuber, and roots. Discard the bad parts and then you can decide if the remaining pieces can be salvaged as leaf, stem, tip, bulb, or tuber cuttings.

Before planting the salvaged parts in a sterile, moist rooting medium such as vermiculite, treat the cut surfaces with a fungicide such as Ferbam or horticultural dusting sulfur. Place to root in a warm, humid situation in bright light but little or no direct sun.

Sudden collapse of a plant may also be caused by overfertilizing, particularly if the fertilizer is applied to bone-dry soil. When this happens, flush out the excess fertilizer by watering heavily several times within a 24-hour period, or by transplanting immediately to a fresh potting mixture.

Have you ever wondered how the prize-winning plants in flower shows can be such perfection, with every last leaf blemish-free, naturally shiny and standing at exactly the right angle in relation to all the rest? Well, I did until my notoriety as a house-plant authority got me invited to judge the amateur classes at the Philadelphia Spring Flower Show. The winning growers invariably brought in plants that had been faithfully groomed on a regular basis beforehand and then given a final spruce-up, including a thorough pot scrubbing, the day before the competition.

In the years since I first judged the Philadelphia, I've come to realize that it isn't necessary to have visions of blue ribbons in your head to make the more cosmetic needs of plants a worthwhile activity. In fact, grooming a healthy but slightly disheveled plant like the spathiphyllum illustrated here is great therapy no matter what your mood.

The first step I take in grooming a plant is to move it into good work light and closely examine all parts to be sure there are no signs of insects that need to be treated. Then I remove all dead leaves, flowers, and stems; some can be picked off, others have tough, fibrous tissue that has to be cut. If leaf tips or edges are discolored, I use scissors to trim off that part and reshape the edge to give it as natural an outline as possible. Then I scrub the pot clean and shower the leaves in tepid water.

I have gradually weeded out my indoor garden so that it is possible for me to groom each plant about once a month. The result has been enormously satisfying; I no longer feel enslaved by a collection of more plants than I have time to enjoy.

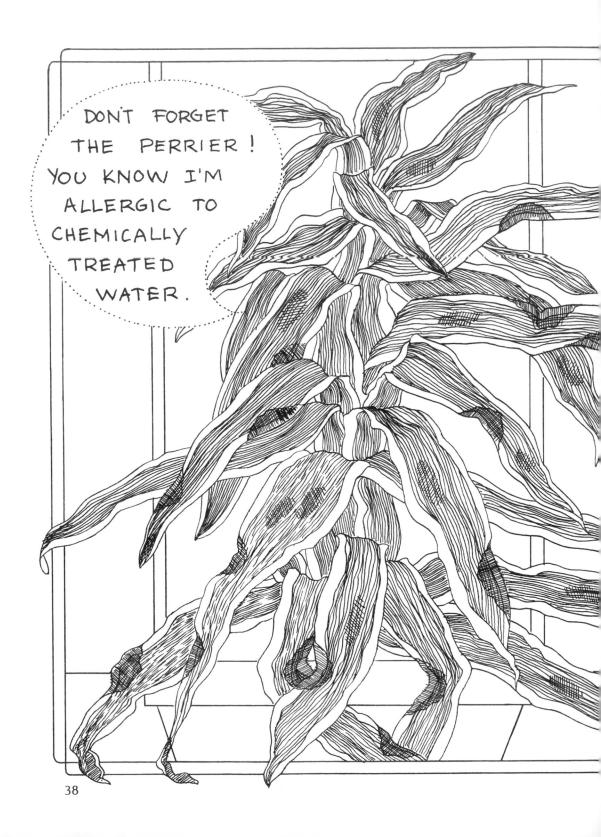

Considering the price of bottled water, I doubt that anyone is going to keep a supply on hand for house plants. However, it is a fact of life that certain plants are highly sensitive to fluoridated and chlorinated water. The *Dracaena deremensis warneckii* illustrated here shows typical damage caused by these chemicals: half-moon dead patches along the leaf margins, and some discolored areas within the leaves. When the leaf tips of chlorophytum or spider plant die, despite your best efforts to keep the soil moist at all times, chemically treated water may be the cause.

Unfortunately, this subject is not as simple as I have implied. Over- or underwatering may result in similar stress signs and so will a buildup in the soil of salts from chemical fertilizers. In parts of Florida, and possibly in other regions, excessive amounts of boron cause the leaves of certain plants, especially those with white variegation, to be discolored. The fact that boron is a natural trace element which plants actually need in infinitesimal amounts adds still further to the confusion.

If you have a plant that shows the stress signs illustrated here, and you are sure that improper watering, fertilizing, or too much boron is not the cause, try this: Use rainwater on your plants. Or, fill a pail, dish pan, or other large container with faucet water and leave it standing open overnight before using on your plants; this will allow most of the harmful gases from fluoridation and chlorination to evaporate. Leaves already damaged will not recover, but new growth should be unblemished.

Another possible solution to this problem is to use water on your plants that has been filtered through one of the purifiers available as a faucet attachment.

There is an old saying to the effect that if you want to grow cacti and other succulents as house plants, watch the weather reports and water them only when it rains in Phoenix. Well, it's an amusing idea, but don't believe a word of it. A wild cactus or other succulent in its native environs has far greater resources for sustenance than one that is confined to a container in an atmosphere that may in effect be drier and warmer than the desert.

Success with cacti and other succulents depends largely on treating them with the same regular attention given rain-forest tropicals and the more temperate-climate herbaceous plants. The chief difference is watering less, at least in the fall and winter months, but not to the point of total desiccation.

Based on my own experiences with cacti and other succulents as house plants, and those of friends who are commercial growers, I suggest this care: Light, directly in a sunny window or with the tops of the plants three to five inches directly beneath three or four fluorescent tubes of the broad-spectrum type, Vita-Lite for example, burned sixteen hours daily. Temperature, average dwelling, but preferably on the cool side in fall and winter (50°–65° F.). Humidity, average dwelling; mist or shower occasionally as a means of keeping the plants clean. Soil, two parts coarse sand to one each of sphagnum peat moss and all-purpose potting soil, plus one heaping tablespoon of bone meal or dolomitic limestone per quart of mixture. Water needs vary, depending on the amount of light and average temperatures, but generally more will be required in spring and summer, less in fall and winter. For best results, use a soil moisture meter, at least to establish a routine of frequency and quantity of watering needed each season.

One of the ironies about gardening indoors is that most plants need to be in or near the windows—which is also where heating and cooling units are usually placed. Present-day forced-air systems used in most post–World War II buildings are not nearly as devastating as steam radiators, but any source of hot or cold air affects the placement of plants within a room.

If you want to grow plants in a window that has a steam radiator beneath it, place a sheet of asbestos or other fireproof insulation material on top of the radiator, then add pebble humidity trays. During coldest weather you may have to add water to the trays twice a day, since the bottom heat quickly evaporates the water.

Be careful not to let any leaves, but especially not thin-textured ones like those of the Boston fern illustrated here, arch downward so that they come in close contact with the radiator itself.

If forced air warms and cools your home or office, simply avoid placing plants directly over the vents. In the winter, pots closest to the source of heat will require extra watering and in the summer they may need less than might be expected, because of the constant breeze of cool air that blows on them. In my own apartment windows, I try to take advantage of the coolest and warmest microclimates in each, which allows me to grow plants in close proximity that actually have quite different temperature requirements.

Excessive room heat is not the only source of damage to plants. Leaves allowed to touch fluorescent tubes or placed too close to an incandescent bulb will develop burned spots just as surely as those that receive too much hot sun. Candlelight becomes plants the same as it does people, but not if the flame is carelessly placed.

There is an old saying to the effect that wherever wandering Jew thrives, money and success are sure to follow. What a nice thought—until your wandering Jew starts dying. Then it's double trauma: a puny plant is no joy to begin with, but what is really unnerving is the nagging thought that the plant may be trying to prepare you for bad times.

Well, take heart, or better yet, take your wandering Jew in hand and calmly figure out what is wrong with it. After all, who wants to tempt fate?

First, compare the symptoms of your wandering Jew against this check list of what it needs in order to thrive. Light, in or near a bright or sunny window; insufficient light causes pale leaves and long, spindly stems. Temperature, average dwelling, ideally a range of 55°–75° F. Humidity, medium (30 percent or more); tolerates less in ideal light and soil that is uniformly moist. Soil, two parts packaged all-purpose potting soil to one each of vermiculite and sand (or perlite); water well, then not again until the surface is beginning to feel dry. If the soil dries out too much, the leaves will wilt and later the tips may die. If the container in which a wandering Jew is hung has no provision for drainage of excess moisture, overwatering can quickly lead to root rot.

Aside from these environmental needs, wandering Jew will grow into a beautiful plant only if the ends of the branches are pinched out following the formation of every three to five new leaves. Otherwise, the branches grow longer and longer, eventually becoming leafless toward the base. In addition, hang the container from a swivel hook and give the plant a quarter turn in the same direction each time you water so that all parts receive an equal amount of light.

IF · · · I · · · WERE

A · · · RICH · · · MAN

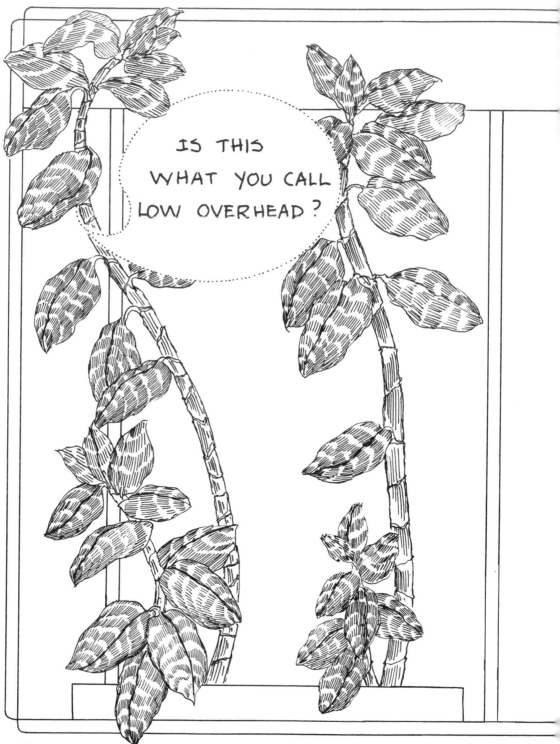

Raise the ceiling or lower the dieffenbachia is a choice you may have to make when your giant dumbcane, like the ones illustrated here, grows entirely too well. Since most of us can't cut a hole in the ceiling and add a skylight in the roof, there is really no choice at all—except to make the plant shorter.

What is disturbing about this problem is that the likely solution requires that drastic action be taken with the plant. If only the top part is cut off, it will likely look decapitated. If there is new growth from the base, any over-sized stems can be cut off near the soil, but this usually leaves a terrible empty spot where we are accustomed to greenery.

The third solution, and the one I recommend, based on my experiences with dieffenbachias and dracaenas, is first to air-layer the parts that need to be removed. When roots form, I have a new plant that immediately replaces part of the foliage to which my eyes have grown accustomed.

The place to make an air-layer along the stem is two or three nodes below the lowermost leaves. Cut a notch about one-third into the stem, surround with a handful of moist, unmilled sphagnum moss, then wrap this with a piece of polyethylene plastic and tie in place, top and bottom. Check the moss once a week for signs of roots and to be sure it is moist; if on the dry side, add water. When strong roots show, make a clean cut through the stem about an inch below and pot up the new plant. If a long piece of bare stem or trunk remains, it can be left in the original pot; new growth may sprout. Or, the stem can be cut off and pieces of it, each with one or more nodes where leaves once grew, set to root, vertically or horizontally, in moist vermiculite.

As beginning gardeners, most of us are taught to repot plants when the soil in which they are growing becomes filled with roots, or at least when roots can be seen coming through the drainage holes and further inspection reveals they have formed a network all around the soil mass.

Then we discover that deciding when to repot is not quite so simple.

For one thing, a network of roots clearly visible does not necessarily mean they have filled the entire soil mass. Roots that are starved for water and nutrients just naturally reach out to the extremes in search of sustenance. And, since repotting in the traditional sense implies moving to a container at least one size larger in diameter, what is one to do about a big plant whose size needs to be limited?

Then there is that nagging worry about the long-range effects of keeping a plant in the same soil where potentially toxic amounts of mineral salts from water and fertilizer may be building up, along with water-purifying chemicals such as chlorine.

Clearly, the time comes when we have to rethink this business of repotting. A kentia palm like the one shown here needs a pot at least two sizes larger, a decision that can be based on aesthetics—a plant that is in proper scale with its container looks stable and balanced. And a cramped plant like this palm looks constricted and top-heavy and probably has to be watered constantly in order to avoid severe drying-out. However, a healthy plant in the right size pot can be repotted right back into it year after year. Just clean the pot and replace most of the old soil with new, having first trimmed a little of the root system and an equal amount of top growth.

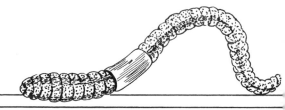

House plants that have spent the summer outdoors often become virtual catchalls for a variety of "creepy-crawlies." The most likely are shown in the illustration opposite, beginning upper left and moving clockwise: ants, spiders, caterpillars, earwigs, millipedes, sowbugs and pillbugs, slugs and earthworms. Since plants that have been outdoors may also be infested with white flies, mealybugs, aphids, thrips, scale, red spider mites and other pests, the only thing to do is clean every plant before bringing it inside.

Handpick or wash away as many of the interlopers as possible, then spray the leaves and stems with an all-purpose pesticide and drench the soil with 50 percent emulsifiable malathion concentrate mixed at the rate of one-half teaspoon to one quart of water (or at the rate recommended on the label).

If you don't want to go to all this trouble, try using an all-purpose systemic applied to the soil. In theory, at least, this treatment should take care of almost everything, both above and below the soil.

If you're strictly an organic gardener, water is the answer, but you'll have to wash the root system thoroughly as well as the leaves and stems, and then repot in equally clean containers using a pasteurized or sterilized soil mixture. This treatment is drastic, especially at a time of the year when the plants have to adjust to reduced light levels, less humidity, and artifical heat. It is safe, however, at least so far as your own health is concerned.

My plants, city apartment dwellers that they are, have on occasion suffered attacks of cockroaches, which eat holes in the leaves. I find roach traps placed among the plants to be fairly effective deterrents.

51

Most of us take for granted that if we lavish good care on a plant that is supposed to bloom, eventually it will produce flowers. But what happens when a plant with healthy leaves and sturdy growth refuses to enter the adulthood of flowering and maturing seeds?

There are several correct answers to this question, depending on which plant is being reluctant. For example, geraniums overfed with nitrogen may not bloom (page 11), Christmas cactus and poinsettias bud when the days are naturally short in autumn (page 62), and desert cacti usually need a period of relative dryness and chilling temperatures in order to flower (page 41).

And then there are bromeliads, like the cryptanthus illustrated here, and the pineapple we eat, not to mention countless other genera, species, varieties, and cultivars, all of which make fascinating house plants. With proper amount of sun or fluorescent light, warmth and humidity, the offsets or "pups" usually grow to flowering size in one to two years. If there is no sign of budding by the time the offset is approximately the same size as the parent, a dose of ethylene gas may be needed to boost bloom.

Fortunately, ethylene gas is not something you have to rush out and buy; it is given off by ripe apples, in particular the varieties Cortland and Jonathan. The treatment is simple: Enclose the bromeliad in a large plastic bag, along with a very ripe apple of one of these varieties (but not a Delicious), then seal the bag. Place in bright light, but no direct sun, or in a fluorescent-light garden. Leave sealed for at least forty-eight hours, preferably seventy-two, then remove the bag and apple and return the bromeliad to where it was growing before. Signs of budding should appear within four to eight weeks; if not, then repeat the treatment as necessary.

Although overheated rooms are probably a thing of the past, the fact remains that when air is warmed, moisture evaporates. And the drier the atmosphere, the more water will be needed in order to maintain satisfactory soil moisture. Even thick-leaved succulents like the various sansevierias or snake plants illustrated here suffer if both the soil and the air are dry and warm at the same time, while thinner-textured foliage like that of impatiens and spider plant is simply doomed.

Well, we all know that Estée Lauder would recommend a moisturizer for dry skin, and what plants need during the winter heating season is a cool-vapor humidifier, used in combination with frequent misting and pebble humidity trays. And for best results, use all three moisturizers; each has its place in nurturing healthy growth. A humidifier is necessary to maintain a constant supply of moisture in the air; and the higher the relative humidity, the warmer you will feel at cooler temperatures. Misting replaces the cleansing, refreshing rains that plants enjoy in nature; it does little to increase humidity. Pebble humidity trays boost the moisture content of the air immediately surrounding the plants, but they are not of much help in humidifying an entire room or house.

Although cacti and other succulents, sansevierias included, do well in low humidity, most plants do best with 40 percent or more. To accurately judge the amount of humidity present in your home, and in the area immediately surrounding your plants, invest in a hygrometer, a convenient indoor gardening accessory that often comes in combination with a thermometer and barometer.

Besides causing older leaves to die prematurely, insufficient humidity necessitates watering more to maintain soil moisture and it can also cause bud drop.

The seedlings illustrated here are plainly starved for light, three of them having already begun to die. This could happen in weak natural light, in or near a window that receives no direct sun, but now that most of us start seedlings in fluorescent-light gardens, it is here that this condition is more likely to occur.

First, if you want to start sturdy seedlings and grow flowering plants such as African violets in a fluorescent-light garden, you'll need a minimum of two 20-watt tubes in a reflector; this unit will light a growing space approximately fifteen to eighteen inches wide and twenty-four inches long. However, a fixture with two 40-watt tubes operates much more efficiently, and gives a growing space up to two feet wide and four feet long. Use a combination of one Cool White and one Warm White tube in each fixture, or any of the broad-spectrum fluorescents advertised for plants. Burn the lights twelve to sixteen hours daily; generally speaking, the warmer the room, the more hours of light needed to foster compact growth.

Second, in order to have a variety of healthy plants in a light garden, it is necessary to group those that need less light toward the ends and sides of the growing area, with the others in the center where they will receive maximum brightness. By the same token, the uppermost leaves of low-light plants can be up to twelve inches from the tubes, while high-light-requiring seedlings need to be boosted up with the tops only three or four inches directly beneath and flowers such as African violets and gloxinias about six to eight inches away. Clean, overturned flowerpots or blocks of wood make convenient boosters.

Plants that you would pinch back regularly to promote compact growth in natural light, such as coleus and geranium, need the same care under fluorescents.

One of the least understood plant problems is the effect of poor light, and lack of sufficient light to nurture growth that is truly healthy and normal plagues most indoor gardeners. There is also widespread confusion about what will *grow* in low light and what will *keep* well in relative dimness before the entire plant begins to go into serious decline.

The schefflera illustrated here makes a good case in point. For years we have been advised that this is a great plant to grow in a dark corner, which it is not. True, a big, healthy schefflera that has been properly conditioned by gradual reductions in light and is absolutely free of red spider mites will keep for several months if not a year or more in a relatively dark place. But the new growth will be spindly, pale green at first, and then it usually turns black, beginning at the leaf tips. In time, quantities of the older leaves may begin to blacken at the tips and fall all over the floor around the plant, a sort of silent protest against light starvation.

If we define low light in relation to plants as being bright enough to read by, then good *keepers* in it include, besides schefflera, philodendron, ferns, spathiphyllum, dieffenbachia, dracaena, screw-pine, and mature bromeliads. Just remember, plants receiving insufficient light need little or no fertilizer and not as much water as they would require under optimum conditions.

To improve the general health of any of these plants, add six to twelve hours of supplementary artificial light daily (one or two 75- or 150-watt floods such as Cool Beam, Cool-Lux or Plant Lite, placed eighteen to thirty-six inches above or to the sides of the plant). Or, move the plant closer to a bright or sunny exposure. In any case, keep the leaves sponged or showered clean with water and maintain moist but not wet or dry soil.

When a plant grows well but fails to meet its usual performance standards, the problem can be puzzling at best and sometimes downright annoying. In the case of a spider plant like the one shown here, the inevitable question is, "Why doesn't it bloom and have babies?" Well, we all know that the delicate, white, lilylike little flowers don't amount to much, but what's the fun of nurturing a spider plant that is perfectly symmetrical and has not a dead leaf in sight unless it also sprouts a healthy cascade of babies?

The truth is, any spider plant that is truly symmetrical and has all green-tipped leaves will eventually have babies. The secret, if there is one, is that the roots need to be slightly potbound. I have read that spider plant is a long-night, short-day bloomer, the same as Christmas cactus and poinsettia, but I also know that my spider flowers and produces lots of babies even though it is lighted twenty-four hours a day.

It is true that a spider plant might not bloom if the soil is too acid, but if this is the case, the leaf tips will probably be brown also. Its proper pH range is supposed to be 6.3 to 6.5; this usually can be achieved by mixing together two parts all-purpose potting soil to one of vermiculite, plus one heaping tablespoon of bone meal to each quart of mix.

It is not true that all-green spider plants have babies and the variegated ones don't, or vice versa. All forms of *Chlorophytum comosum* proliferate by means of long flowering stems which not only bear seeds but also give birth to baby plants; these include the plain species, as well as *vittatum* (shown), with a white stripe down the center, and *variegatum*, which has white margins. Miniature spider, *C. bichetii,* resembles a young Variegatum, but it does not send out airborne babies.

The effect day length has on flowering can be one of the most confusing aspects of growing house plants, but it needn't be if certain basics are understood. Although the more scientific aspects of gardening are fraught with exceptions, generally speaking, the plants we grow indoors for flowers may be divided into three groups with regard to their response to light:

(1) Long-night (short-day)—for example, Christmas cactus, kalanchoe, poinsettia, and chrysanthemum.

(2) Short-night (long-day)—for example, tuberous begonias and China aster (callistephus).

(3) Indeterminate, the kinds that bloom at any season when the environment fosters active, healthy growth—for example, semperflorens begonia, African violet, gloxinia, geranium, and impatiens.

The plants in groups two and three seldom present any problems with regard to bloom, unless, of course, you try to grow tuberous begonias or China-asters in the winter, in which case supplementary artificial light will be needed at night. However, the long-night, short-day plants in group one, Christmas cactus for example (illustrated), are not likely to bloom if they receive more than twelve hours of light daily, natural or artificial, in September, October, and November.

In other words, if you want your Christmas cactus, poinsettia, and kalanchoe to bloom for the holidays, be sure they receive no artifical light at night, from sundown to sunup, in autumn. The important thing to remember is that even brief periods of light during the dark period may prevent flowering. To succeed with Christmas cactus, you'll also need to withhold fertilizer during this season, water only enough to keep the leaves firm, and try to provide a cool place where temperatures average around 60° F.

As beginners, most of us are thankful just to get something green to grow from an avocado pit; never mind that it grows willy-nilly, with leaves and stems in all the wrong places. Then one day the truth dawns: If we can grow it to this stage, why not go all the way and train a shapely bush or tree?

Well, in most cases the thing to do is leave the old avocado to grow by whim and start from scratch with a new pit. Here's the procedure I follow: Fill a six-inch pot with a mixture of two parts packaged all-purpose potting soil to one each of sphagnum peat moss and sand (or perlite). Snuggle the rounded base of the pit into the soil in the center of the pot, leaving at least half of the pit exposed. Moisten well, then place to grow in any bright or sunny situation; water often enough to keep the soil moist; try not to let it be either soggy-wet or bone-dry.

The moment to decide whether you are going to train a bush or tree comes when the sprout is eight inches tall. To grow a tree, follow this procedure: (1) Set a three- to four-foot stake in the pot right next to the pit. As the sprout grows taller, tie it loosely to the stake, using short strips of green plastic (but not with wire embedded in them). If any side branches begin to develop, remove. (2) When the single stem reaches the top of the stake, pinch out the tip. (3) In the future, nip out the tip of every new branch that grows, as soon as it forms three or four leaves. (4) Each time you water, give the pot a quarter turn in the same direction so that all sides will receive equal light. (5) When the head is established, remove all leaves from the trunk.

To grow a bushy avocado, follow this procedure: When the sprout is eight inches tall, cut it back to six; follow steps (3) and (4) above.

Until a few years ago, the prayer plant was rarely seen outside of botanical gardens and in the collections of devoted plantpeople. Now it has become one of the most widely distributed of all house plants, the sort of thing you can pick up almost anywhere, including supermarkets, dimestores, and discount chains. Despite all this popularity, which certainly indicates that the prayer plant has a strong will to live, I rarely see one that is truly well-grown, with all the leaves properly colored and no yellow or brown tips.

Prayer plant, a species of *Maranta,* grows wild in Brazilian rain forests where constant moisture at the roots, high humidity, and warmth are the rule. As a house plant, it adapts remarkably well to low humidity and temperatures between 60° and 80° F. What usually causes the leaves to yellow at the tips and then shrivel up and die prematurely is allowing the soil to dry out too much between waterings. When this happens repeatedly, red spider mites often move in for the kill.

If you have a maranta in this condition, I suggest you cut it back, following this procedure: Remove the pot and crumble away most of the soil. Trim off dead, broken, or discolored roots. Cut off, right at the base, any long stems with dead leaves along them. Repot the roots and any remaining new growth emerging from the base in a mixture of equal parts all-purpose potting soil, sphagnum peat moss, vermiculite, and sand (or perlite). Keep constantly moist in a warm, bright spot, but in little or no direct sun. In a few weeks' time, healthy new growth should sprout from the roots.

Meanwhile, if the stems you cut off have healthy growth at the tips, remove the dead leaves and treat the remaining parts as cuttings which you can root in a pot of vermiculite, then transplant to a soil mix.

When aphids attack a plant, there is little mistaking their presence, at least not for long, because they multiply rapidly, soon covering tip growth and flower buds. According to my references, there are lots of different kinds of aphids, sometimes called plant lice, in various colors, but I can't remember ever seeing any that were not green. Since the plant parts on which they dine are mostly in some shade of green, it is not always easy to detect their presence before damage is done, the result being malformation of both flowers and new leaves.

An unchecked infestation of aphids usually leads to the potentially more serious problem of black sooty mold on the foliage, especially on the larger, older leaves toward the bottom of the plant. What happens is that the sweet honeydew substance excreted by the aphids collects on the leaves, thus making them a fail-safe landing field and breeding ground for disease spores. Unless the mold is checked by spray treatments with a fungicide, defoliation is almost inevitable.

When you detect the presence of aphids on a potted plant, the quickest, most direct means of control—and a surprisingly effective one—is to wash them down the sink, tub, or shower drain, using a fairly brisk spray of tepid water. Leave the plants to dry, but before you return them to the growing area, check to be sure you didn't miss any aphids. Repeat treatment as necessary.

Aphids are also fairly easy to control with almost any all-purpose insecticide sold for use on house plants. Pyrethrin, for example, one of the most widely used organic poisons for controlling sap-sucking insects, is a surefire aphid killer. Favorite hosts include Chinese hibiscus (illustrated), rose, chrysanthemum, calceolaria and cineraria, but given the time, aphids will spread to almost every plant indoors, orchids included.

Have you every fallen asleep at the beach and slept so long that whatever exposed parts facing up burned to a crisp? Well, the very day this sort of thing is likely to happen to us is also when house plants can get a bad case of sunburn. Thin-leaved kinds like the rex begonia illustrated here are extremely sensitive to a sudden increase in the intensity and duration of direct sunlight, just as a fair-skinned person is.

One way to avoid this kind of damage to a plant is never to leave it in direct sun when the soil is dry. When the roots have an ample supply of moisture, they are much better able to sustain the top growth through periods of hot sun and warmer temperatures. However, if the plant has been growing in relatively low light, no amount of water in the soil can prevent damage to the leaves if they are suddenly exposed to full, direct sun for several hours.

Late spring is the time when plants are most likely to suffer sunburn, usually during the period between winter heating and summer air conditioning. If leaves wilt or have a lackluster appearance even though the soil is moist, move the pots back from the window or provide some shade, either from a thin curtain or a venetian blind.

If you put your house plants outdoors for the duration of warm, frost-free weather, gradually accustom them to increasing amounts of sun even though they may have been growing inside in a sunny exposure. At first move them where they receive only early morning or late afternoon sun and protection from strong winds, perhaps on a porch or under a shade tree. After a week or two it will be safe for them to be in more sun.

No matter how green your thumb is, if you garden long enough and grow a variety of different plants, eventually one of them will fail despite your best efforts. What is important is to recognize what is worth doctoring and what isn't. If the case is hopeless, the sooner you get rid of the ailing plant, the better. Otherwise, the very sight of it is depressing and it may contaminate other, healthy plants.

The *Dizygotheca elegantissima* or false aralia illustrated here makes a good case in point. Although this plant has been known to adapt to a wide variety of conditions, it has also been known to die or, perhaps worse, simply to linger. And a dizygotheca that needs more or less light, water, humidity, warmth, fresh air, or fertilizer may hang on to life for months or years before the last leaf shrivels up and dies.

If you have a dizygotheca, or almost any other plant for that matter, which has not appeared to be in good health for a long time, drastic action may be the best course. Examine the leaves and stems. If you detect red spider mites, mealybugs or other insects, decide if the general health of the ailing plant warrants or even permits treatment. Unless there are some healthy leaves and stems, discard everything except the pot, which can be cleaned and used again.

If you decide to try to save the plant, remove the pot and crumble away all the old soil with your fingers; then wash the root system in tepid water. Trim off any dead, broken, or discolored roots. Wash the leaves and stems until you can detect no signs of any insect. Cut off any dead or diseased leaves and stems. Repot in fresh soil and lavish the best care possible on your patient. If it grows, you will have saved a plant. If it dies, you did your best; allow no feelings of guilt.

There are many reasons why a plant like the lipstick vine illustrated here forms flowerbuds that grow with great promise for a period of time and then drop off or turn brown. The most common is allowing the soil to dry out too much at a critical stage, but a sudden chill, especially when the soil is very wet, will cause the same problem, as will over-fertilizing, small amounts of gas escaping from a range or heater, or a poorly ventilated room filled with cigarette smokers.

Insufficient amounts of either sunlight or fluorescent light causes bud drop in some plants, lipstick vine and gloxinia in particular, even though the foliage appears healthy. By the same token, lack of humidity may prevent flowering despite the fact that buds have developed.

A sudden reduction in the amount of light to which a plant is accustomed almost invariably causes buds to die, the most vulnerable being specimens brought from a greenhouse into a warmer environment where there is also less humidity and fresh air. This often happens to florist plants such as cyclamen, azalea, gloxinia, Rieger begonia and African violet, but also fuchsia, ivy-leaf geranium, hydrangea, and lantana.

Although ripe apples are sometimes used to force mature bromeliads into bloom (page 52), placing a bowl of them in close proximity to a flowering plant such as the lipstick vine can have quite the opposite effect: the ethylene gas they give off can cause bud drop. However incongruous it may seem, the heavy, intense fragrance of hyacinths in full bloom may cause the same problem, especially within the confines of a small room that is not well ventilated.

If you have grown a plant to the bud stage, but no flowers open, check also for signs of insects such as mealybugs, aphids and red spider mites.

Most house plants that receive adequate light don't need a stake in order to stand up and look their best. However, sometimes a well-placed support of just the right shape and appearance can make the difference between success and failure, both visually and culturally. The amaryllis shown here is deceptively beautiful, thanks to the artistry of Lauren Jarrett. It is more usual for an amaryllis that cannot stand up straight to fall out of the pot and come crashing to the floor, which is not a pretty sight at all.

The way to avoid this problem with an amaryllis, or with any other plant that seems top-heavy or insecure in the pot, is to provide a stake as soon as possible, preferably before the stems have grown crooked or otherwise unnaturally shaped. In the case of an amaryllis, staking should be needed only at flowering time; if subsequent leaf growth is too weak to stand on its own, the plant is not receiving enough sunlight or the bulb has failed to establish its roots.

There are three types of staking I do, each designed to meet a particular need: (1) To support a stem not strong enough to carry the weight of its flowers, an amaryllis or a phalaenopsis orchid, for instance, I use a piece of heavy wire with a loop bent at one end to cradle the stem, and long enough to insert in the soil to the bottom of the pot. The wire can be straight or curved just so, to give support without causing an awkward appearance. (2) For a single-stemmed tall plant or something like a tree-form geranium I use a sturdy bamboo or wood stake, securing the two with lengths of half-inch-wide dark green plastic. (3) For a bushy plant with several stems, I add three or four small bamboo stakes equidistant around the pot and tie with dark green twine.

Some plants that send up offsets from or near the base of the parent, Boston fern for example, can be left alone indefinitely, or until you want to increase your stock. In the case of clivia and eucharis, the thing to do is give them a fairly large pot, say eight inches in diameter, and then leave the bulbs to multiply until they are crowded; otherwise, flowering is not likely.

However, when the mature plant bearing an offset is a bromeliad, like the variegated pineapple (*Ananas comosus va riegatus*) illustrated here, division is in order as soon as the two seem to be crowding each other. Follow this procedure: Remove the pot and crumble away most of the growing medium so that you can examine the entire root system and determine exactly where to cut the two apart so as to retain as many roots as possible on the offset or "pup," which is what most bromeliad growers call one of these.

Next, pot up each in its own container, using your own bromeliad growing medium, or a mixture of equal parts packaged all-purpose potting soil, sphagnum peat moss, sand (or perlite), and coarse vermiculite. Place in bright light, but little or no direct sun, until new growth indicates that the roots are established.

Water thoroughly and then not again until the soil at the surface feels almost dry. Keep the cup formed by the leaves filled with fresh water and mist the foliage once or twice a day, especially during the winter heating season. Whether the parent grows again, sends up another offset, or goes into terminal decline depends largely on its natural habit, a highly variable factor influenced not only by the kind of bromeliad, but also by its age and environmental conditions at the time of division. The popular Silver King aechmea, for example, usually blooms, sends up offsets, and then dies.

While most house plants do not go underground or stop growing entirely at any time of the year, most of them do need less water and little or no fertilizer during late fall and winter while the days are short. Plants growing in a warm, humid, fluorescent-light garden are of course an exception; their water and fertilizer needs remain fairly constant year round.

However, plants which grow from a bulb or tuber, like the caladium illustrated here, usually require a season of rest annually. The length and time of this dormant period varies, depending on the natural habitat of the plant and whether or not it requires the long-light days of spring and summer or the relatively short-light days of fall and winter to trigger leaf and flower growth. In cultivation, very few of these plants will go dormant unless you stop fertilizing and watering them following a period of active growth. This is called "drying off." When the soil becomes dry enough, the leaves will wilt, turn yellow and dry up, at which time you can remove them, either by cutting or giving a slight tug at the base. Then the pot can be stored in a dark, dry place at moderate temperatures (50°–65° F.).

If storage space is limited, the bulb or tuber can be removed from the soil and stored in a cup or two of vermiculite placed in a plastic bag in which a few holes have been cut to facilitate air circulation. Whether they are left in the pots of soil or stored in vermiculite, keep the medium barely damp or almost dry—but not bone-dry. The intention is to provide only enough dampness to keep the bulb or tuber firm, or to prevent shriveling, but not so much moisture that premature sprouting or rotting is encouraged. After a rest of two to four months, repot in fresh soil and return to a suitable growing environment.

Since plants in nature do not grow in pots, it is no easy matter to explain why pot size is so important to their success in cultivation. Obviously, it is difficult for an enormous plant to live in a very small pot, but why shouldn't a small plant thrive in a big pot? After all, if it had sprouted in the middle of a field, the roots would have no restrictions, at least not in theory. In reality, of course, plants in nature often have to fight for root space as well as light, air, and water.

One of the problems that often occurs when a small plant is given a large pot is that the soil tends to hold too much water, especially if the container is made of plastic, glazed ceramic, or any other material that is nonporous. The advantage, in this case, of using unglazed clay is that approximately equal amounts of water evaporate through the walls of the pot and the surface soil. It follows, then, that if you water carefully, there is really no reason not to use a large pot for a small plant, presuming that the combination is pleasing to your eyes.

However, if the plant you are growing needs to be rootbound in order to bloom, as in the case of the hoya or wax plant illustrated here, it will pay to match it to as small a pot as possible. Hoya specialist Loyce Andrews grows each rooted cutting in an eight-ounce foam cup until after it blooms the first time, then she recommends transplanting to a four- or five-inch pot.

Another popular plant that needs to be at least slightly rootbound in order to bloom is the African violet; as a general rule, the width of the pot should equal one-half to two-thirds the diameter of the leaves. Clivia and eucharis lily should be left in the same eight- to ten-inch pot for several years; simply replace some of the old soil with fresh annually.

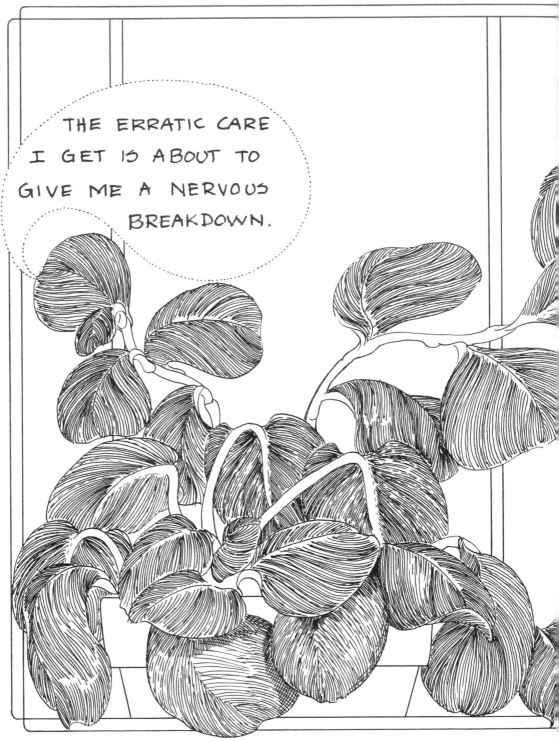

Although innumerable things can go wrong with a plant, in most cases it boils down to feast or famine—too much or not enough water, heat, light, humidity, fresh air, or fertilizer. In the case of the peperomia illustrated here, the soil has been allowed to become so dry between waterings that older leaves and stems have wilted and fallen over the edge of the pot. Since the stems in particular of the peperomia are succulent and water-filled, once they wilt, it is not usually possible for them to assimilate moisture again. As a result, they die.

Peperomias and semperflorens or wax begonias are especially sensitive to over- and underwatering. Unfortunately, their watering needs vary, depending mostly on average temperatures at the time, but also on the amount and intensity of light. As a general rule, when temperatures are on the cool side (below 70° F.), the growing medium needs to be kept on the dry side; when average temperatures are warm (above 70° F.), they can take more water. If the plant is growing in less than ideal light, or during a period of cloudy weather, it will need less water.

These same general rules hold for fertilizing peperomias, semperflorens begonias, and other plants with water-filled stems. It is fine to fertilize them every two weeks, following label directions, during warm, sunny weather, but during periods of low light and cool temperatures, they should not be fertilized.

Plants like peperomias and semperflorens begonias are most easily handled if they are planted in unglazed clay pots filled with a porous medium made by mixing together equal parts packaged all-purpose potting soil, sphagnum peat moss, vermiculite, and sand (or perlite). Do not leave the pot standing in a saucer of water.

The primary rule to remember about fertilizing is to do it only when the plant is in a general state of good health, new growth is apparent, and the soil is nicely moist. Spring and summer are the usual times for most plants cultivated in natural light, but those in a fluorescent-light garden may be fertilized all year.

If you are using a fertilizer with which you are not familiar, try it first on a few plants and mix precisely according to directions on the label. If the plant is a recent acquisition, examine the surface soil for signs of timed-release fertilizer pellets; if you detect their presence, apply no fertilizer of any kind for at least three months.

There are several schools of thought about frequency of fertilizing. Some growers fertilize plants in active growth every two weeks. Others, especially those who grow in a soil-less mix (usually based on sphagnum peat moss, perlite, and vermiculite), feed a little with every watering, mixing the fertilizer at approximately one-fourth to one-fifth the strength recommended on the label for fertilizing every two weeks. And finally, some gardeners prefer the convenience of fertilizing with timed-release pellets which have to be applied only three or four times a year.

Regardless of the type fertilizer or frequency of application, be cautious about overdoing. Plants that are highly vulnerable to excessive fertilizer include ferns and begonias in general, but also kinds with watery stems such as peperomia and thin-textured leaves like the Trileaf Wonder syngonium illustrated here. The growing medium of any plant fertilized regularly with a chemical fertilizer should be flushed out with clean water every few months, and once a year, most of the old soil should be replaced with fresh.

When the leaves of a plant turn brown at the tips and along the edges, most of us are quick to conclude that we're over- or under-watering, the light is too weak or too strong, there are too many chemicals in the water or, God forbid, maybe it's red spider mites again. Well, all of these things happen to plants all the time, but occasionally one like the areca palm illustrated here is perfectly healthy except for the fact that it has been placed too close to pedestrian traffic. Leaves that are constantly being brushed, bruised, and torn by people passing too close are bound to develop a raggle-taggle appearance.

Sometimes the solution is as simple as moving the plant a foot or two in the right direction. In the case of an average-sized palm four to six feet tall, the answer may be to boost it up on a low table, pedestal, or stool so that the main girth of the foliage will be out of the line of traffic. Often this placement also creates a more decorative effect, simply by raising the fronds so that they arch gracefully overhead rather than at shoulder height.

When mechanical damage results in dead tips or edges, the thing to do, of course, is to scissor-trim back to healthy tissue, leaving as natural a leaf shape as you can. Stems that have been bent but not completely broken may be saved by careful staking.

When you shop for plants, it pays generally to avoid any that show signs of mechanical damage: broken leaves or stems; holes poked or torn in the foliage, possibly by careless placement next to a thorny cactus; wobbly growth that seems poorly rooted or is unstable in the pot. If close inspection reveals that a lot of the leaves have been scissor-trimmed along the edges and tips to remove damaged parts, it may be better to select another plant that hasn't required a facelift.

Despite what you may have read or been told, the Norfolk Island pine does not make a good Christmas tree, at least not if this means hanging ornaments on the branches, or worse yet, stringing electric lights on them. Ornaments tend to weight the branches down into a permanent droop and lights are likely to burn some of the needles. Unfortunately, since the Norfolk pine is a woody evergreen, once needles or branches are damaged, they will not grow back to their former state.

Rather than burden a Norfolk pine with decorations, leave it as is, a celebration of nature without any trimmings. What you can do to give it a more festive appearance is to place the utilitarian pot in which it grows inside a basket or decorative cachepot. Here's the procedure: Select an attractive container that is slightly larger in diameter and a half-inch or so taller than the pot. Place a waterproof saucer in the bottom, then position the pot inside. For a pleasing finishing touch, carpet the soil and hide the pot rim by spreading florist's sheet moss across the surface. Add a bow if you like, and arrange gifts all around, but if you really care for the health of your Norfolk pine, leave it to grow in exactly the same environment to which it is accustomed.

When the branches of Norfolk pine droop for no apparent reason, insufficient light may be the cause. When needles shrivel and die along the branches, check the soil; it should feel moist, not soggy-wet and never bone-dry. A combination of dry soil, low humidity, and temperatures over 70° F. during the winter heating season is almost sure to invite red spider mites; combat by correcting the environment and showering the plant almost daily with tepid water. If mites persist, spray as necessary with a miticide such as Kelthane.

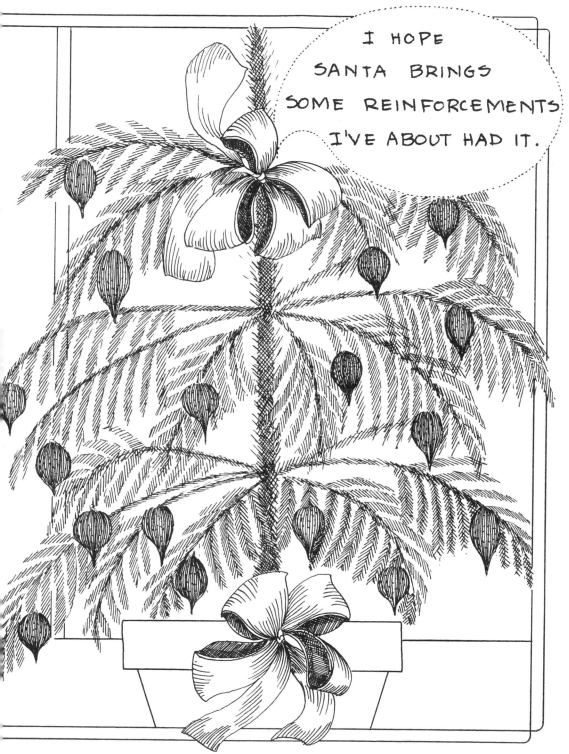

When the leaves of a plant turn yellow overnight, the cause may be gas escaping from a kitchen range, a hot water heater, or furnace. Cyclamen, illustrated here, geranium, Jerusalem cherry, Christmas pepper, and tomato are extremely sensitive; within the confines of a small kitchen, for example, where there is little ventilation, even the small amount of gas that escapes from a defective pilot light will turn these plants yellow within a matter of hours. Once the damage is done, there is little to do except prune off the affected parts, stop the gas leak—and hope for recovery.

There are, of course, other air pollutants that can cause damage to house plants. Before painting a room, for example, move all the plants elsewhere so that they will not be subjected to a concentration of the fumes. Delicate ferns and budding plants just about to bloom may suffer in the cigarette smoke given off by a standing-room-only cocktail party. And the ethylene gas produced by a bowlful of ripe apples can cause flowerbuds to die on some plants; on the other hand, a ripe apple is sometimes exactly what the doctor ordered to coax a mature bromeliad into bloom (see page 52).

All of these situations point up the need for giving house plants fresh air that circulates freely. Without it, the likelihood of insect and disease problems increases substantially. Unfortunately, those of us who live in or near urban and industrial areas are only too aware of the scarcity of air that is fresh—and polluted air is no better for plants than it is for us. It is thought to prevent achimenes from blooming, may cause bud blast in some varieties of gloxinia and generally declining health in many plants. The bad effects of air pollution can be offset in part by keeping leaves clean and by providing the best general care possible.

Large-bodied cacti occasionally develop an area of diseased tissue at or near the soil line, as illustrated here. Sometimes the cause is simply overwatering, especially during the fall and winter months when temperatures are likely to be on the cool side and light levels are reduced.

However, the disease organisms that lead to black rot of this type are always present in the atmosphere. All they need to get a foothold is a broken place on any part of the cactus, the body itself, or the roots, where poor drainage or lack of fresh air circulation prevents excess moisture from drying quickly. The roots or the skin of a cactus can be wounded in transplanting, by a sudden gust of wind that topples the pot, or by a sharp-edged stone placed too close to the body. Occasionally an attack of mealybugs left unchecked for too long may also lead to serious disease problems.

The minute you discover any part of a cactus body that is unnaturally soft, shrunken, or discolored, try to determine the extent of damage. If only a small area of the body is affected, use a sharp knife to remove the diseased portion, trimming back to tissue that is obviously healthy. Then place the plant in a well-ventilated growing area where a constant supply of fresh air will keep the wound dry until a callus forms a natural seal against disease.

If you discover that the root system or a major part of the cactus body is diseased, make a clean cut above the rotted portion. Place the salvaged cutting on a counter or shelf where dry air circulates freely. As soon as a callus forms on the cut surface, prop up the cutting with the base just touching damp sand; pot up when roots begin to form.

Not all plant problems stem from an improper environment or attacks of various pests or diseases. The piggyback illustrated here is a good case in point. No matter how well you care for it, eventually the time comes when the old plant is spent and should be discarded; but not before you have rooted some of the baby plants which grow on top of the old leaves.

Although we think of piggyback as a house plant, it grows wild along the Pacific Coast from northern California all the way to Alaska. In fact, it can survive temperatures as low as 10° F. In nature, it is the habit of this plant literally to walk away from itself by means of the babies, the weight of which pulls the base of the parent leaf into contact with moist soil. In time each of these forms a mature plant with leaf-bearing babies and the process is repeated. In this way, the plant perpetuates itself, always reaching out to fresh, fertile soil.

The time to start a piggyback baby is before the parent is obviously going into decline. The procedure is simple: Press the base of a plant-bearing leaf into a small pot of moist soil placed alongside the parent. As soon as the baby is making active growth, cut the stem that connects it to the old plant.

To grow a healthy piggyback of any age, use a growing medium rich in moisture-holding humus; for example, equal parts packaged all-purpose potting soil, sphagnum peat moss, and vermiculite. Water often enough to keep evenly moist at all times; dryness to the point of causing piggyback to wilt may set it into irreversible decline, not to mention inviting an attack of red spider mites which can be equally devastating. Give piggyback bright light but little or no direct sun, ideally in a moist, cool (50°–70° F.) atmosphere.

If you want to grow cacti and other succulents whose ancestors lived in the drier climates of the world, be prepared to give them lots of direct sunlight or a spot directly beneath three, and preferably four, fluorescent tubes of the broad-spectrum type, Vita-Lite, for example. When these plants are starved for light, the new growth, if any, will be spindly and may bear small resemblance to the parts that grew in ample sun. For example, instead of thick, rounded pads, the prickly-pear cactus (*Opuntia*) sends up thin pads barely a half inch across; these grow longer and longer until they turn into strangely malformed vines.

Jade plant, illustrated here, is much more tolerant of low light than most succulents, but if left for long periods of time in dimness, it will stretch into pale, increasingly smaller stems and leaves. If the daylight is bright enough to read small print by, a fairly decent jade can be nurtured by pinching out the branch tips after each grows two or three sets of leaves, by giving the pot a quarter turn in the same direction each time you water, so that all parts receive equal light, by keeping the soil on the dry side, and by fertilizing very little.

If you have to bring a sizable cactus or other succulent into much less light than that to which it is accustomed, water it with great caution. Your chances for success will be vastly increased if you use a soil moisture meter with a probe long enough to check deep in the pot, under the body of the plant. Many times, the sandy soil in which succulents are usually planted will feel completely dry on top while an inch or two down it is damp if not wet. It will also help if you can summer your plant outdoors in ample light, but move it gradually into full sunlight and water more.

Most house plants grow best in fresh air that circulates freely. Without it, insect and disease problems are likely to be much more troublesome. However, when temperatures outdoors fall below 60° F., take care that no plant native to the tropics is situated in a chilling draft. The episcia or flame violet illustrated here is especially sensitive; a sudden change from cozy warmth to temperatures of 55° F. or less can cause it to wilt and die almost overnight.

The leaves of plants placed too close to the panes of a window or greenhouse also run the risk of being burned in hot weather and frozen in the winter. Obviously, desert cacti and other succulents will tolerate more heat than a leafy plant from tropical rain forests, and cold-hardy plants like English ivy, piggyback and strawberry-geranium don't mind a chill. But when growth comes in direct contact with either very hot or very cold glass or plastic, there is bound to be some physical damage.

As a rule, it pays to keep all growth at least four inches back from any kind of window, glass or plastic. This space permits air to circulate freely between the two. In times of extreme heat or cold, a small oscillating fan placed strategically can prevent the buildup of motionless pockets of air that could freeze or burn plant parts.

If you are uncertain about the air temperatures around your plants, invest in a good thermometer, ideally a maximum/minimum type that will allow you to determine the highs and lows within a given period of time. At any season when temperatures are colder than desirable, it is generally best to keep the soil drier than usual; by the same token, more water is likely to be needed during periods of excessive heat.

As indoor gardeners, one of the most frustrating things that can happen to any of us is to have a thrifty plant suddenly go limp for no apparent reason. Instinct tells us first to check the soil; if the surface feels bone-dry, we breathe a sigh of relief; what this plant needs is a good soaking with tepid water. If the surface feels wet and soggy, we know that overwatering has probably led to root rot, which is by no means good news, but at least we can hope to salvage some healthy cuttings (see page 34).

But when the surface soil feels perfectly moist, determining what is wrong may not be so easy. It could be overfertilizing, a draft of very hot or very cold air blowing directly on the plant, a serious attack of soil mealybugs or nematodes on the root system, or an attack of insects on the leaves and stems that has gone undetected for too long.

Unfortunately, a plant that wilts suddenly for no obvious reason may also have fallen victim to a party guest who has laughingly—and thoughtlessly—shared an alcoholic beverage with it. If you suspect this might have happened, as it has to the pteris or Victorian table fern illustrated here, smell the soil. If the odor is sour or in any way unpleasant, remove the pot and crumble away as much of the soil as you can with your fingers, then wash the roots clean in a strong stream of tepid water. Trim off any roots that are discolored, broken, or obviously dead, then replant in fresh, sterilized potting soil. Set the pot to soak in a shallow basin of water; when beads of moisture show on the soil surface, set aside to drain. Finally, return the plant to where it was growing before, but protect from hot, direct sun until the leaves and stems are firm and growing healthily as before.

Having pots of tulips, hyacinths, daffodils, and crocus blooming indoors weeks if not months before spring weather brings them en masse outdoors is easy, provided the bulbs have formed strong root systems before forcing begins. Obviously, the hyacinth illustrated here is not well rooted. Failure could mean that the bulb was allowed to dry out after roots had begun to grow; that temperatures were too warm; or merely that insufficient time was allowed for the roots to form.

Although hyacinths and crocus may be rooted and brought to bloom in water, all spring bulbs, these included, perform best when planted in ordinary clay or plastic bulb pans. Pot them up any time between late September and Thanksgiving.

Add a layer of broken pot shards or pebbles in the bottom of each pot for drainage. Fill to 1½ inches from the top with a mixture of two parts packaged all-purpose potting soil to one each of sphagnum peat moss and vermiculite. Add as many bulbs as you can so they almost touch; fill pot with soil and firm gently, leaving the bulb tips exposed. Water thoroughly; label each pot.

Now place the potted bulbs in a cool (40°–50° F.), dark place; most require ten to twelve weeks for rooting. Be sure the bulbs never dry out, that mice cannot get to them, and that they are not subjected to freezing temperatures. Good places to root bulbs outdoors include a cold frame or trench; cover with plastic foam, then mulch. Indoors, bulbs can be rooted in a refrigerator with the thermostat set high enough so that there is no danger of their freezing.

When strong roots show through the pot drainage holes, forcing can begin, first in a semidark place for one to two weeks at 55°–60° F., then in bright window or fluorescent-light garden at 55°–70° F.

Beautiful plants that say nice things, like the African violet and phalaenopsis orchid illustrated here, are the reward for learning how to interpret nature's sign language. Gardening offers satisfactions at many levels, but hardly any equals that of knowing that you have recognized a plant in stress, properly interpreted the problem, and solved it.

In fact, until you know the troubles of plants and what causes them, it is difficult to appreciate properly one that is perfection. Scotland, for example, is renowned for the superb gardeners it produces, despite a difficult climate. Or should we say "because of" the difficult climate? Personally, I find it encouraging to know that it is possible to grow beautiful plants even though the environment may be far from ideal.

Growing plants, like the practice of medicine, is an inexact science. And "practice" is a good word to keep in mind as you garden. We live in a time when most of us grow plants as a means of recreation, as therapy and as a sport. The result of this activity should be an ever-increasing sense of well-being, but it won't happen unless you really dig in and learn from your mistakes. If you want to become a good gardener, take it seriously, the same as you would learning to cook or play tennis. And by "seriously," I don't mean to imply that any of these activities is a bore; learning for the fun of it is an idea whose time has come, along with the graying of America, which is clearly indicated by the upward movement of the median age. We are going to live longer and remain active decades beyond earlier generations. Gardening, both indoors and outdoors, is an activity suited to all ages and almost all circumstances. It is high adventure, the thrill of discovery, and 100 percent natural. I believe in it.

A Selected Bibliography

Ballard, Ernesta D. *The Art of Training Plants*. New York: Barnes and Noble, 1974.

———. *Garden in Your House*. New York: Harper & Row, 1971.

Baylis, Maggie. *Practicing Plant Parenthood*. San Francisco: 101 Productions, 1975.

Elbert, Virginie and George. *The House Plant Decorating Book*. New York: Dutton, 1977.

———. *Plants That Really Bloom Indoors*. New York: Simon & Schuster, 1974.

Fenton, Dx. *Greenhousing for Purple Thumbs*. San Francisco: 101 Productions, 1976.

Fitch, Charles Marden. *The Complete Book of Houseplants Under Lights*. New York: Hawthorn, 1975.

Graf, Alfred. *Exotic Plant Manual*. East Rutherford, N.J.: Roehrs, 1970.

Guest, C. Z. *First Garden*. New York: Putnam, 1976.

Heriteau, Jacqueline. *The Office Gardener*. New York: Hawthorn, 1977.

Hirsch, Doris F. *Indoor Plants: Comprehensive Care and Culture*. Radnor, Pa.: Chilton, 1977.

Kramer, Jack. *Plants That Grow on Air*. New York: Simon & Schuster, 1975.

———. *Growing Orchids at Your Windows*. New York: Hawthorn, 1976.

McDonald, Elvin. *The Greenhouse Gardener*. New York: New American Library, 1975.

———. *The House Plant Answer Book*. New York: Popular Library, 1975.

————. *House Plants to Grow If You Have No Sun.* New York: Popular Library, 1975.

————. *How to Grow House Plants from Seed.* New York: Mason/Charter, 1976.

————. *Little Plants for Small Spaces.* New York: M. Evans, 1974.

————. *Plants as Therapy.* New York: Praeger, 1976.

————. *The World Book of House Plants,* Revised Edition. New York: Funk & Wagnalls, 1975.

Mulligan, William C. *Cacti and Succulents.* New York: Grosset & Dunlap, 1975.

Ortho Books. *House Plants Indoors/Outdoors.* San Francisco: Ortho Book Division, 1974.

Skelsey, Alice, and Mooney, Cecile. *Every Room a Garden.* New York: Workman Publishing, 1976.

Sunset Books. *How to Grow African Violets.* Menlo Park, Calif.; Lane Publishing, 1977.

————. *Gardening in Containers,* 1977.

Taylor, Kathryn S., and Gregg, Edith W. *Winter Flowers in Greenhouse and Sun-Heated Pit.* New York: Scribners 1969.

Yang, Linda. *The Terrace Gardener's Handbook.* Garden City, N.Y.: Doubleday, 1975.

By-Mail Sources for Plants, Supplies, and Equipment

Although local nurseries, shops, and garden centers carry a wide variety of plants and the supplies needed for their care, one of the most exciting aspects of gardening is reading and dreaming over the catalogs of mail-order specialists. These offer a ready, convenient source for virtually every plant in cultivation, plus highly specialized tools, equipment, and supplies.

The list that follows is by no means all-inclusive; inclusion is no more an endorsement than exclusion is condemnation. Over the years I have purchased plants and other materials from most of these firms and have almost always been pleased. I have also had the pleasure of visiting many of the nurseries and greenhouses listed, an experience I highly recommend.

Abbey Garden, 176 Toro Canyon Road, Carpinteria, California 93013. Cacti and other succulents. 50 cents for catalog.
Abbot's Nursery, Route 4, Box 482, Mobile, Alabama 36609. Camellias.
Alberts & Merkel Brothers, Inc. 2210 S. Federal Highway, Boynton Beach, Florida 33435. Orchids, tropical foliage, and flowering plants. 75 cents for list.

Antonelli Brothers, 2545 Capitola Road, Santa Cruz, California 95062. Tuberous begonias, gloxinias, and achimenes.

Louise Barnaby, 12178 Highview Street, Vicksburg, Michigan 49097. African violets. Send stamp for list.

Mrs. Mary V. Boose, 9 Turney Place, Trumbull, Connecticut 06611. African violets and episcias. 15 cents for list.

John Brudy's Rare Plant House, P.O. Box 1348, Cocoa Beach, Florida 32931 Unusual seeds and plants. $1.00 for catalog.

Buell's Greenhouses, Weeks Road, Eastford, Connecticut 06242. Complete listing of gloxinias, African violets, and other gesneriads; supplies. $1.00 for catalog.

Burgess Seed and Plant Company, 67 East Battle Creek, Galesburg, Michigan 49503. Plants, bulbs, seeds.

W. Atlee Burpee Company, Warminter, Pennsylvania 18974. Seeds, bulbs, plants; supplies.

David Buttram, P.O. Box 193, Independence, Missouri 64051. African violets. 10 cents for list.

Cactus Gem Nursery, 10092 Mann Drive, Cupertino, California (visit Thursday–Sunday); by mail write P.O. Box 327, Aromas, California 95004.

Carobil Farm and Greenhouses, Brunswick, Maine 04011. Catalog of geraniums.

Castle Violets, 614 Castle Road, Colorado Springs, Colorado 80904. African violets.

Champion's African Violets, 8848 Van Hoesen Road, Clay, New York 13041. African violets. Send stamp for list.

William Collier Orchids, Tissue Culture Laboratories, 6701 Cahuilla, Riverside, California 92509.

Cook's Geranium Nursery, 714 N. Grand, Lyons, Kansas 67544. Geraniums. 25 cents for catalog.

Davis Cactus Garden, 1522 Jefferson Street, Kerrville, Texas 78028. 25 cents for catalog.

DeGiorgi Company, Inc., Council Bluffs, Iowa 51504. Seeds and bulbs.

P. DeJager and Sons, 188 Asbury Street, South Hamilton, Massachusetts 01982. Bulbs.

L. Easterbrook Greenhouses, 10 Craig Street, Butler, Ohio 44822. African violets, other gesneriads, terrarium plants; supplies. $1.25 for catalog.

Electric Farm, 104 B. Lee Road, Oak Hill, New York 12460. Gesneriads. Send self-addressed, stamped envelope for list.

Farmer Seed and Nursery Company, Faribault, Minnesota 55021. Seeds, bulbs, plants.

Fennell Orchid Company, Inc., 26715 S.W. 157th Avenue, Homestead, Florida 33030. Orchids; supplies.

Fernwood Plants, 1311 Fernwood Pacific Drive, Topanga, California 90290. Rare and unusual cacti.

Ffoulkes, 610 Bryan Street, Jacksonville, Florida 32202. African violets, 25 cents for list.

Henry Field Seed and Nursery Company, 407 Sycamore, Shenandoah, Iowa 51061. Plants, bulbs, seeds; supplies.

Fischer Greenhouses, Linwood, New Jersey 08221. African violets and other gesneriads. 25 cents for catalog.

Fox Orchids, 6615 W. Markham, Little Rock, Arkansas 72205. Orchids; supplies.

Arthur Freed Orchids, Inc., 5731 S. Bonsall Drive, Malibu, California 90255. Orchids; supplies.

J. Howard French, P.O. Box 87, Center Rutland, Vermont 05736. Bulbs.

Girard Nurseries, P.O. Box 428, Geneva, Ohio 44041. Bonsai materials.

Golden Plant Nurseries, Inc., 7300 Astro Street, Orlando, Florida 32807. 25 cents for list.

Grigsby Cactus Gardens, 2354 Bella Vista Drive, Vista, California 92083. Cacti and other succulents. 50 cents for catalog.

Gurney Seed and Nursery Company, Yankton, South Dakota 57078. Seeds, bulbs, plants.

Orchids by Hausermann, Inc., P.O. Box 363, Elmhurst, Illinois 60126. Orchids; supplies. $1.25 for catalog.

Helen's Cactus, 2205 Mirasol, Brownsville, Texas 78520. Cacti and other succulents. 10 cents for list.

Henrietta's Nursery, 1345 N. Brawley Avenue, Fresno, California 93705. Cacti and other succulents. 20 cents for catalog.

Hilltop Farm, Route 3, Box 216, Cleveland, Texas. Geraniums and herbs.
Sim T. Holmes, 100 Tustarawas Road, Beaver, Pennsylvania 15009. African violets, miniatures and regular.
Spencer M. Howard Orchid Imports, 11802 Huston Street, North Hollywood, California 91607. Unusual orchids.
Gordon M. Hoyt Orchids, Seattle Heights, Washington 98036. Orchids; supplies.
Margaret Ilgenfritz Orchids, Blossom Lane, P.O. Box 665, Monroe, Michigan 48161. Orchids; supplies. $1.00 for catalog.
Jones and Scully, Inc., 2200 N.W. 33rd Avenue, Miami, Florida 33142. Orchids; supplies. $3.50 for catalog.
K & L Cactus Nursery, 12712 Stockton Blvd., Galt, California 95632.
Kartuz Greenhouses, 92 Chestnut Street, Wilmington, Massachusetts 01887. Gesneriads, begonias, house plants in general; supplies. 50 cents for catalog.
Kirkpatrick's, 27785 De Anza Street, Barstow, California 92311. Cacti and other succulents. 10 cents for list.
Kolb's Greenhouses, 724 Belvedere Road, Phillipsburg, New Jersey 08865. African violets. Send stamp for list.
Lauray, Undermountain Road, Route 41, Salisbury, Connecticut 06068. Gesneriads, cacti, and other succulents, begonias. 50 cents for catalog.
Logee's Greenhouses, 55 North Street, Danielson, Connecticut 06239. Complete selection of house plants, with special emphasis on begonias and geraniums. $1.00 for catalog.
Paul Lowe, Mt. Vernon Springs, North Carolina 27345. Begonias. 25 cents for catalog.
Lyndon Lyon, 14 Mutchler Street, Dolgeville, New York 13329. African violets and other gesneriads.
Mary's African Violets, 19788 San Juan, Detroit, Michigan 48221. African violets; supplies.
Earl May Seed and Nursery Company, Shenandoah, Iowa 51603. Seeds, bulbs, plants.
Rod McLellan Company, 1450 El Camino Real, South San Francisco, California 94080. Orchids; supplies.

Merry Gardens, Camden, Maine 04843. House plants and herbs, large selection of begonias and geraniums. $1.00 for catalog.

Mini-Roses, P.O. Box 245, Station A, Dallas, Texas 75208. Miniature roses.

Modlin's Cactus Gardens, Route 4, Box 3034, Vista, California 92083. Cacti and other succulents. 25 cents for catalog.

Cactus by Mueller, 10411 Rosedale Highway, Bakersfield, California 93308. Cacti and other succulents. 10 cents for list.

Nor'east Miniature Roses, 58 Hammond Street, Rowley, Massachusetts 01969.

Nuccio's Nurseries, 3555 Chaney Trail, Altadena, California 91001. Hybrid camellias and azaleas.

Orinda Nursery, Bridgeville, Delaware 19933. Hybrid camellias.

George W. Park Seed Company, Inc., Greenwood, South Carolina 29647. Seeds, bulbs, plants; supplies.

Penn Valley Orchids, 239 Old Gulph Road, Wynnewood, Pennsylvania 19096. Orchids.

Rainbow Begonia Gardens, P.O. Box 991, Westminster, California 92683.

Routh's Greenhouse, Louisburg, Missouri 65685.

John Scheepers, Inc., 63 Wall Street, New York 10005. Flowering bulbs.

Sequoia Nursery, 2519 East Noble Street, Visalia, California 93277. Miniature roses.

Shadow Lawn Nursery, 637 Holly Lane, Plantation, Florida 33317. Seeds and cuttings. 50 cents for catalog.

Shaffer's Tropical Gardens, Inc., 3220 41 Avenue, Capitola, California 95010. Orchids.

P. R. Sharp, 104 N. Chapel Avenue #3, Alhambra, California 91801. South American and Mexican cacti.

R. H. Shumway Seedsman, Rockford, Illinois 61101. Seeds, plants, bulbs.

Singers' Growing Things, 6385 Enfield Avenue, Reseda, California 91335. Succulents.

Small World Miniature Roses, P.O. Box 562, Rogue River, Oregon 97537.

Smith's Cactus Garden, P.O. Box 871, Paramount, California 90723. Cacti and other succulents. 30 cents for list.

Fred A. Stewart, Inc., 1212 East Las Tunas Drive, San Gabriel, California 91778. Orchids; supplies.

Stokes Seeds, 737 Main Street, Buffalo, New York 14203. Seeds.

Ed Storms, 4223 Pershing, Fort Worth, Texas 76107. Lithops and other succulents.

Sunnybrook Farms, 9448 Mayfield Road, Chesterland, Ohio 44026. Herbs, scented geraniums, many other plants.

Sunnyslope Gardens, 8638 Huntington Drive, San Gabriel, California 91775. Chrysanthemums.

Thompson & Morgan, Inc., P.O. Box 24, Somerdale, New Jersey 08083. Seeds of many unusual plants.

Thon's Garden Mums, 4815 Oak Street, Crystal Lake, Illinois 60014. Chrysanthemums.

Tinari Greenhouses, Box 190, 2325 Valley Road, Huntingdon Valley, Pennsylvania 19006. African violets, gesneriads; supplies. 25 cents for catalog.

White Flower Farm, Litchfield, Connecticut 06759. Spectacular English hybrid tuberous-rooted begonias, other plants and bulbs. $3.50 for catalog.

Walther's Exotic House Plants, R.D. #3, Box 30, Catskill, New York 12414.

Wilson Brothers, Roachdale, Indiana 47121. House plants, with special emphasis on geraniums.

Plant Societies and Periodicals

American Begonia Society, Inc., 139 North Ledoux Road, Beverly Hills, California 90211. *The Begonian* (monthly).

The American Bonsai Society, 953 South Shore Drive, Lake Waukomis, Parksville, Missouri 64151. *Bonsai* (quarterly) and *ABStracts* (interim monthly newletter).

Bonsai Clubs International, 445 Blake Street, Menlo Park, California 94025.

The Bonsai Society of Greater New York, Inc., Box E, Bronx Park, Bronx, New York 10466. *The Bonsai Bulletin* (quarterly).

Bonsai Society of Texas, Box 11054, Dallas, Texas 75235.

Bromeliad Society, Inc., P.O. Box 3279, Santa Monica, California 90403. Regional chapters in the South and New York. *The Bromeliad Journal* (six times a year).

Cactus and Succulent Society of America, Inc., Box 167, Reseda, California 91335. *Cactus and Succulent Journal* (bimonthly).

Cymbidium Society of America, Inc., 6787 Worsham Drive, Whittier, California 90602. Two branch chapters. *Cymbidium Society News.*

Epiphyllum Society of America, 218 East Greystone Avenue, Monrovia, California 91016. *Epiphyllum Bulletin.*

American Fern Society, Biological Sciences Group, University of Connecticut, Storrs, Connecticut 06268. *American Fern Journal* (quarterly).

Los Angeles International Fern Society, 2423 Burritt Avenue, Redondo Beach, California 90278. *Newsletter* and annual magazine.

Flower and Garden Magazine, 4251 Pennsylvania Avenue, Kansas City, Missouri 64111. Monthly magazine. Gardening indoors/outdoors.

The American Fuchsia Society, Hall of Flowers, Golden Gate Park, San Francisco, California 94122.

National Fuchsia Society, 10934 East Flory Street, Whittier, California 90606. *The National Fuchsia Fan* (monthly).

International Geranium Society, 11960 Pascal Avenue, Colton, California 92324. Five regional chapters. *Geraniums Around the World* (quarterly).

The American Gesneria Society, 11983 Darlington Avenue, Los Angeles, California 90049. *Gesneriad Saintpaulia News* (bimonthly).

The American Gloxinia/Gesneriad Society, Inc., P.O. Box 1974, New Milford, Connecticut 06776. *The Gloxinian* (bimonthly).

The American Hibiscus Society, Box 98, Eagle Lake, Florida 33139. *Seed Pod* (quarterly).

The American Horticultural Society, River Farm, Mount Vernon, Virginia 22121. *News and Views* newsletter (six times a year). *American Horticulturist* magazine (six times a year).

Horticulture, 300 Massachusetts Avenue, Boston, Massachusetts 02115. Monthly magazine. Gardening indoors/outdoors.

The Indoor Light Gardening Society of America, Inc., 423 Powell Drive, Bay Village, Ohio 44140.

American Orchid Society, Inc., Botanical Museum of Harvard University, Cambridge, Massachusetts 02138. *American Orchid Society Bulletin.*

Organic Gardening and Farming, Emmaus, Pennsylvania 18049. Monthly magazine. Gardening organically, indoors/outdoors.

The Palm Society, 1320 South Venetian Way, Miami, Florida 33139. Five chapters. *Princepes* (quarterly).

The American Plant Life Society, The American Amaryllis Society Group, Box 150, La Jolla, California 92037. *Plantlife-Amaryllis Yearbook* (bulletin).

Plants Alive, 1255 Portland Place, Boulder, Colorado 80302. Monthly magazine. Gardening indoors.

Saintpaulia International, Box 10604, Knoxville, Tennessee 37919. *Gesneriad Saintpaulia News* (bimonthly).

African Violet Society of America, Inc., Box 1326, Knoxville, Tennessee 37901. *African Violet Magazine* (five times a year).

Index